Adult Coloring Book
Valentine's Day

Coloring Books for Adults

Auntie V. 's

Awesome Stress Relief Patterns

Featuring Less Detail and Fresh New Designs

By: V. PEREIRA

Adult Coloring Book
Valentine's Day

Coloring Books For Adults

Auntie V.'s

ISBN-13:978-1523366736

SBN-10:1523366737

Visit us online:

FACEBOOK: https://www.facebook.com/auntievscoloringbooksforadults/

AUTHOR CENTRAL: https://www.amazon.com/author/auntiev

BLOG: https://auntievs.wordpress.com/

TWITTER: @AuntieVs

DEDICATION

To Gary, whom without, this book
would never have been possible.

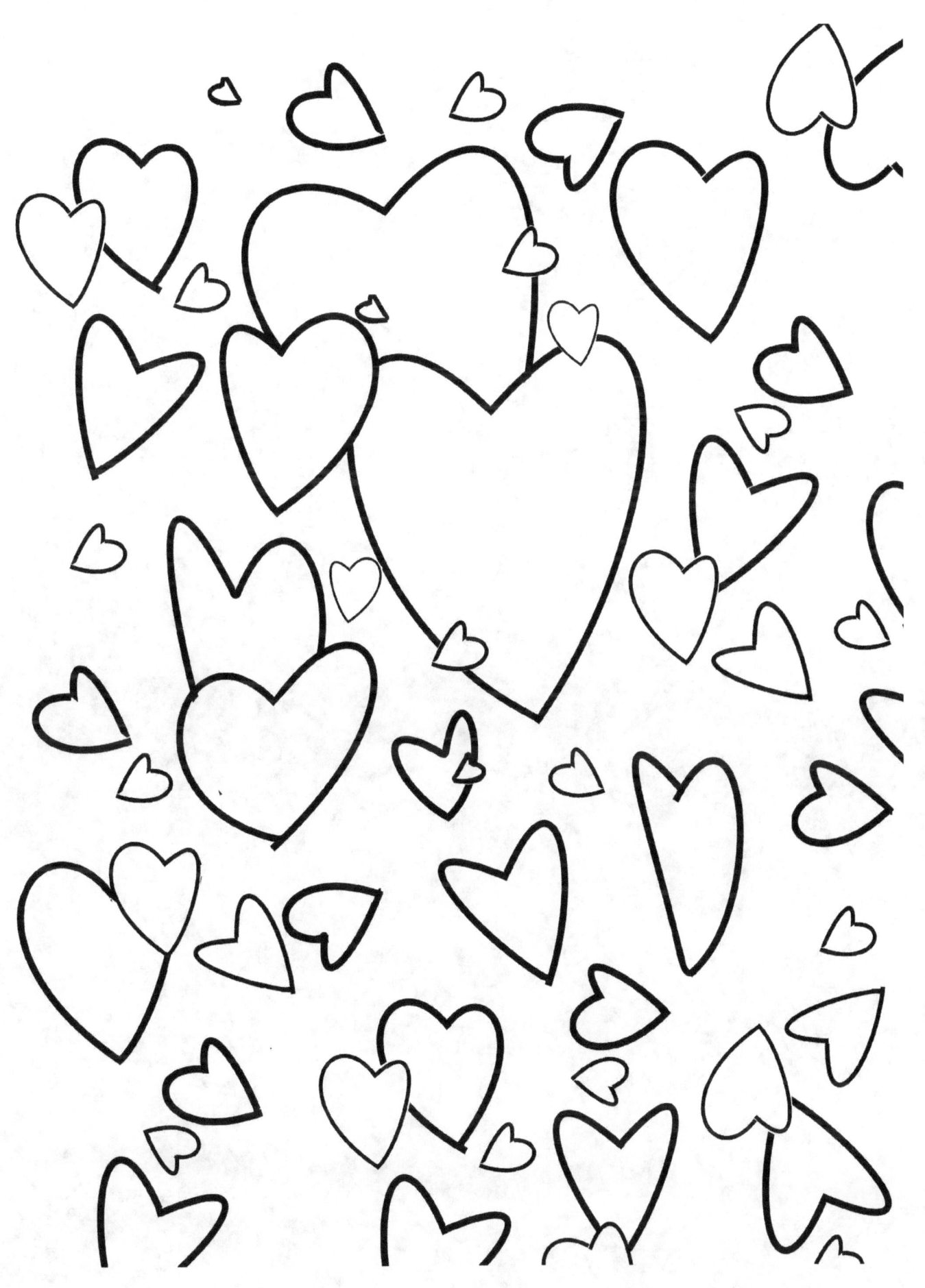

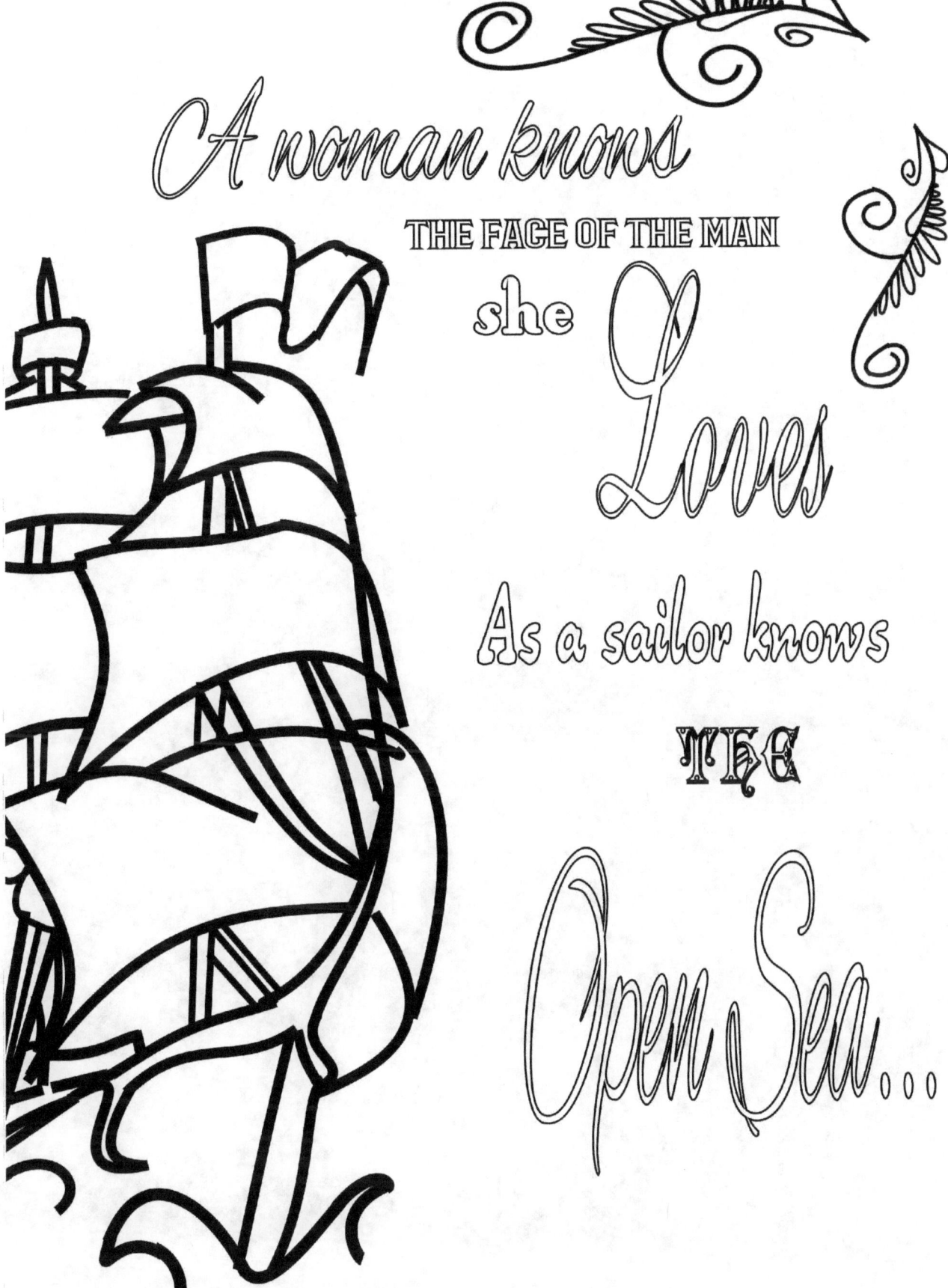

A woman knows THE FACE OF THE MAN she Loves As a sailor knows THE Open Sea...

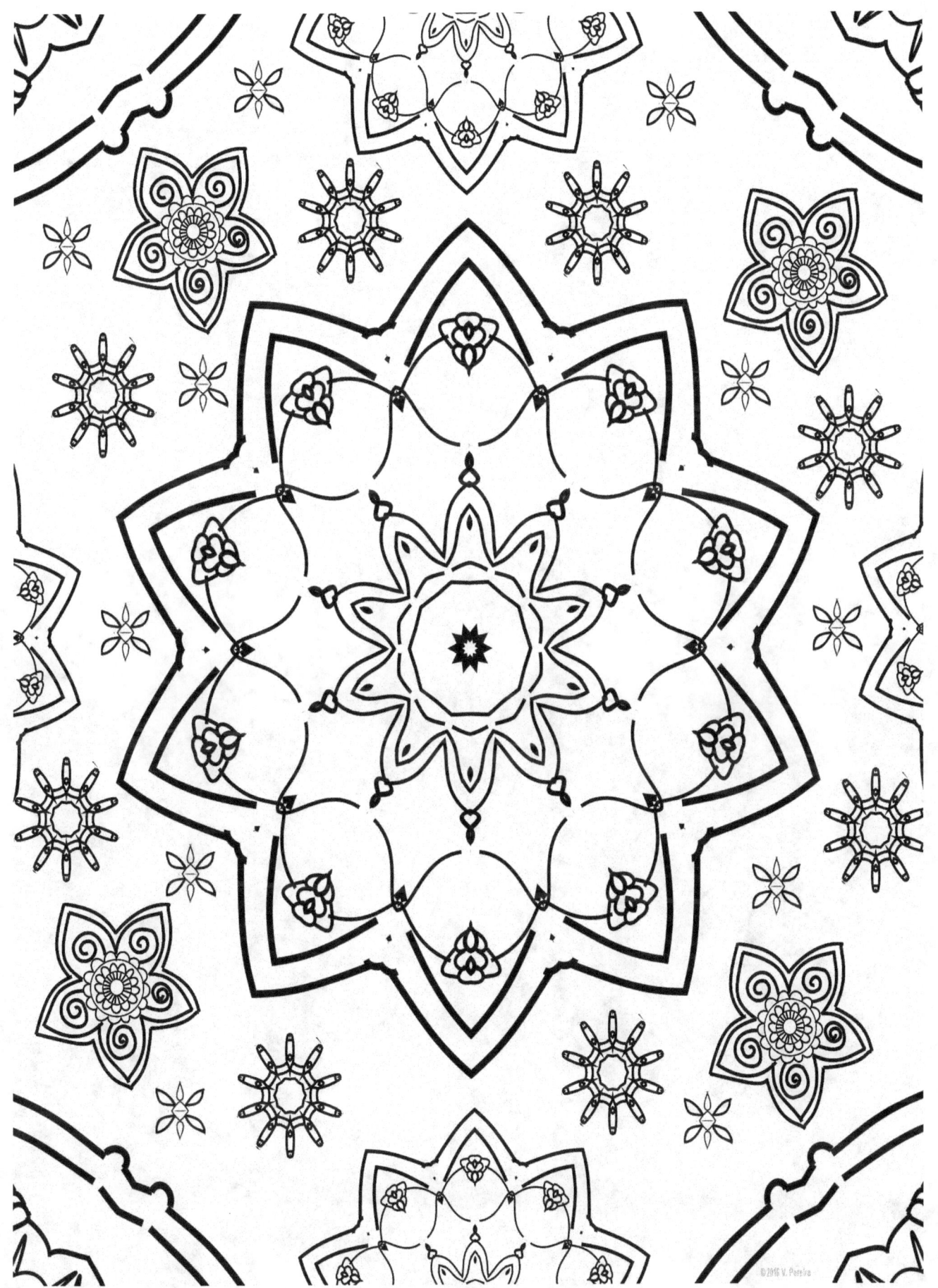

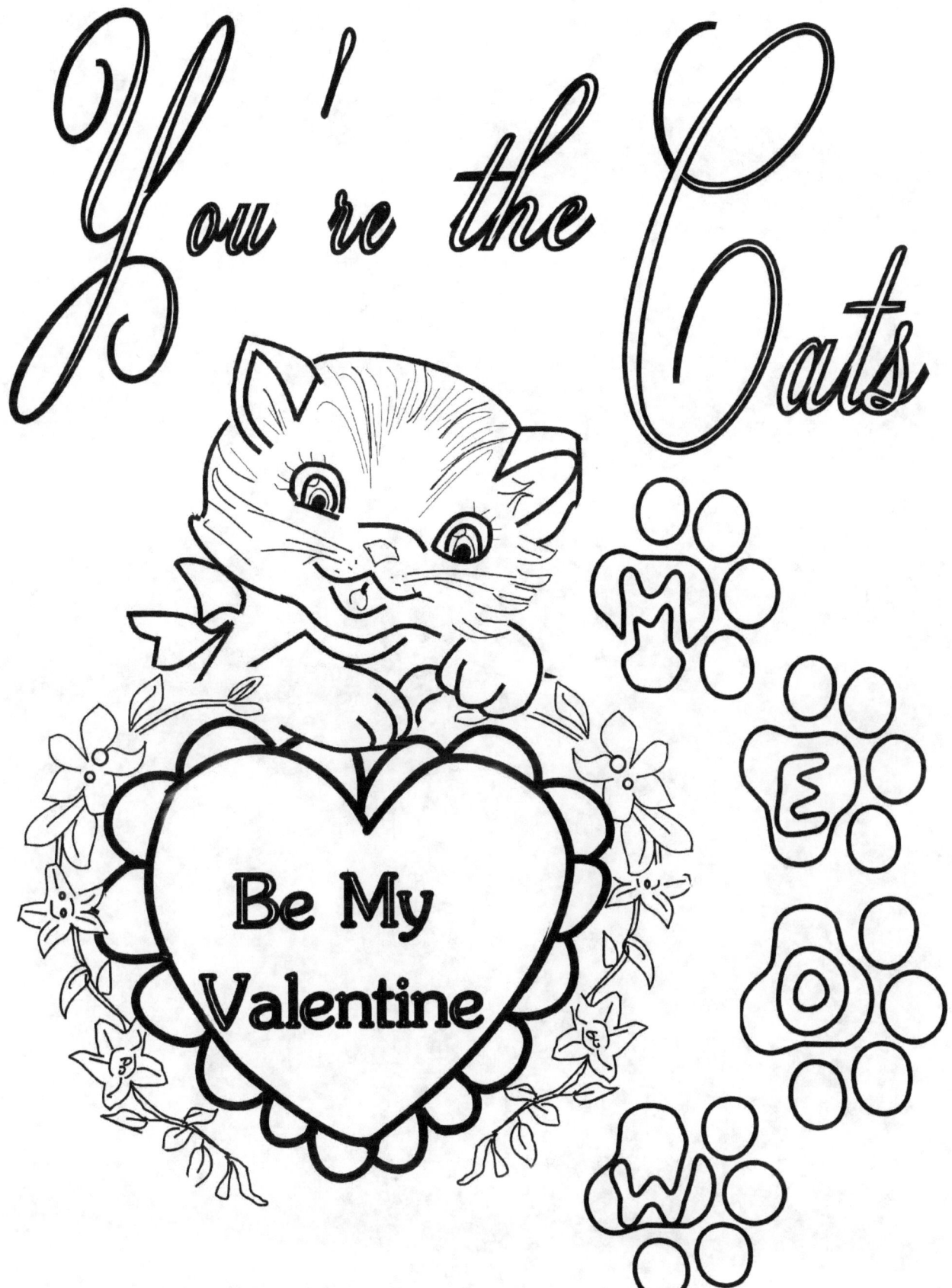

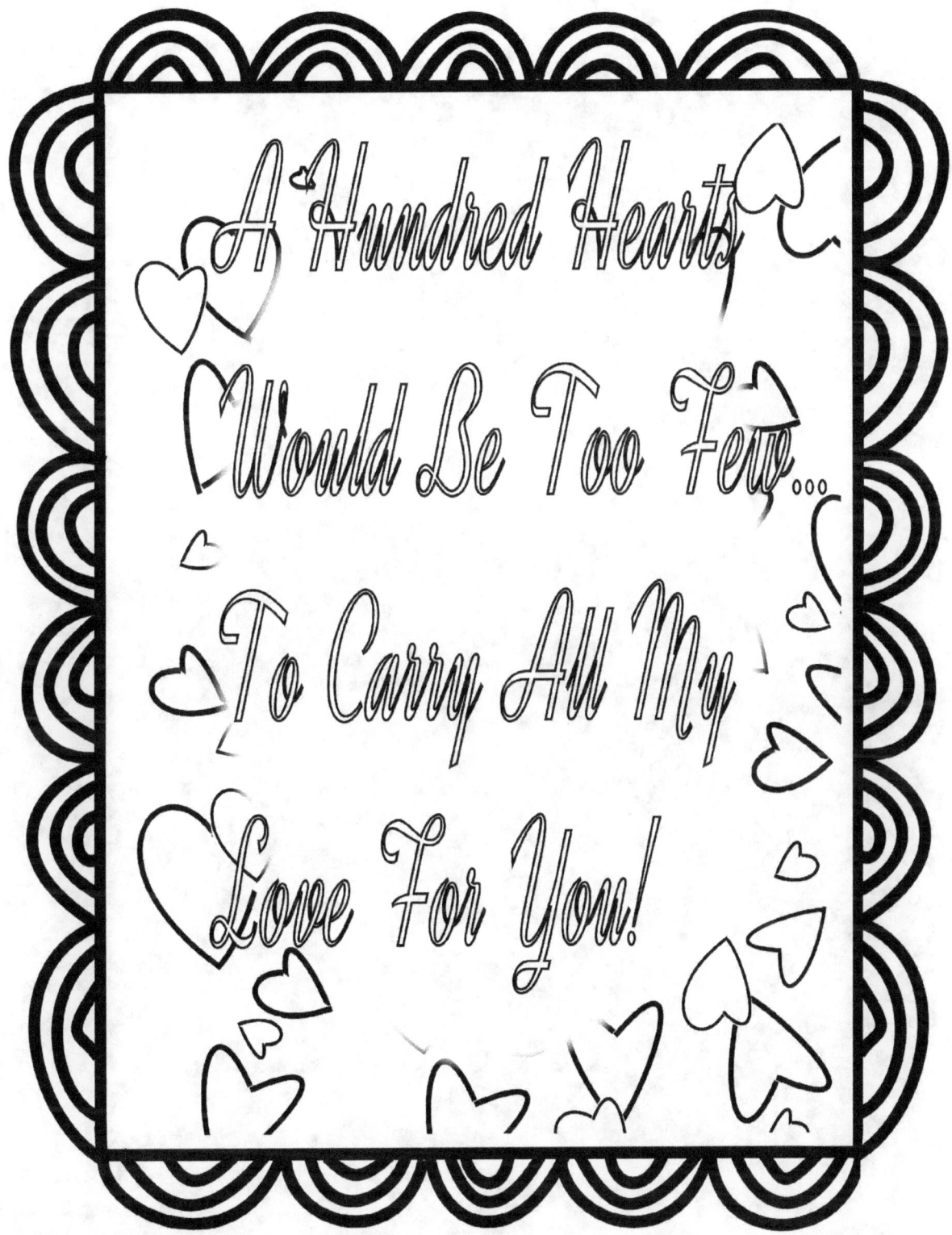

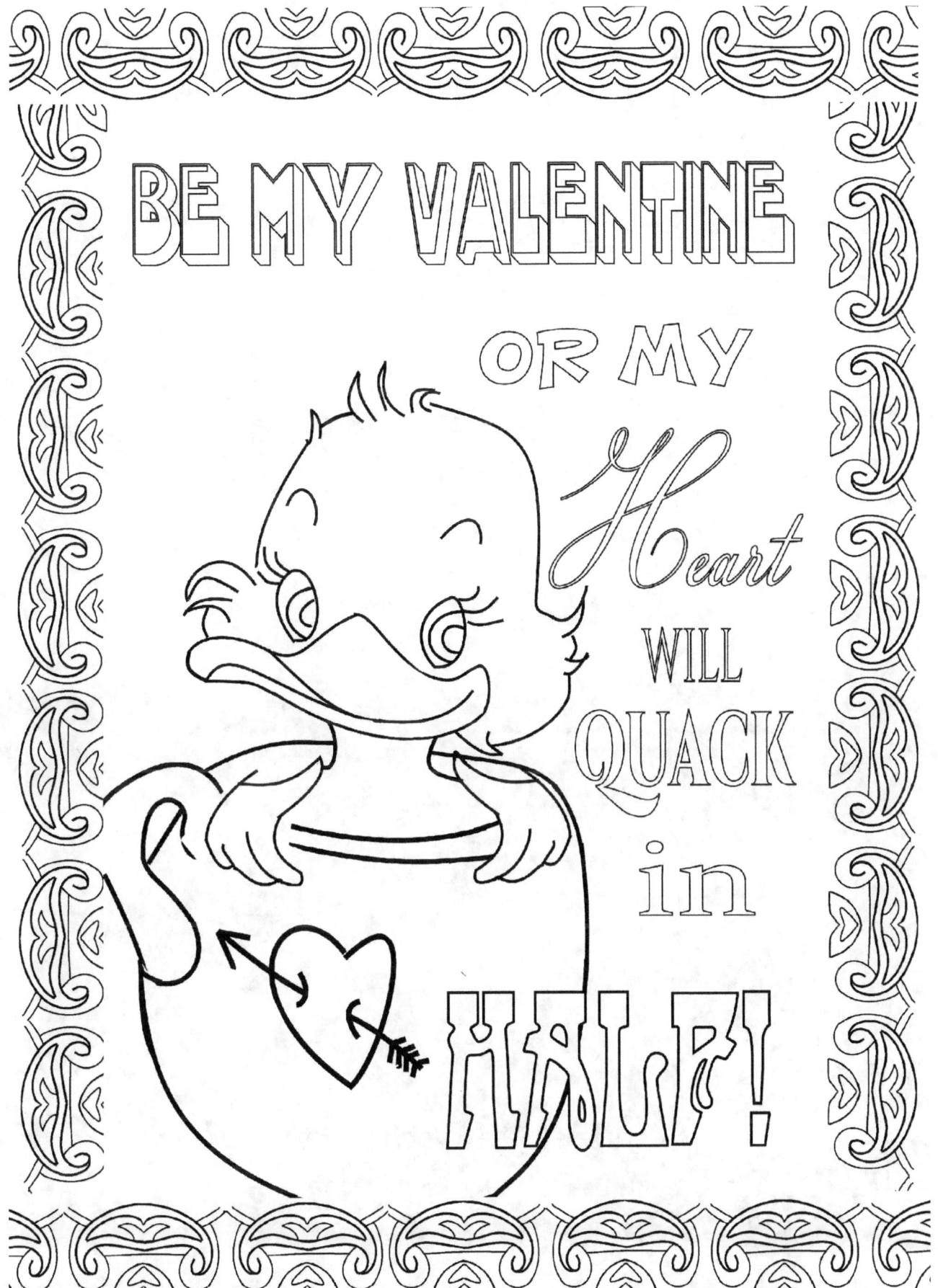

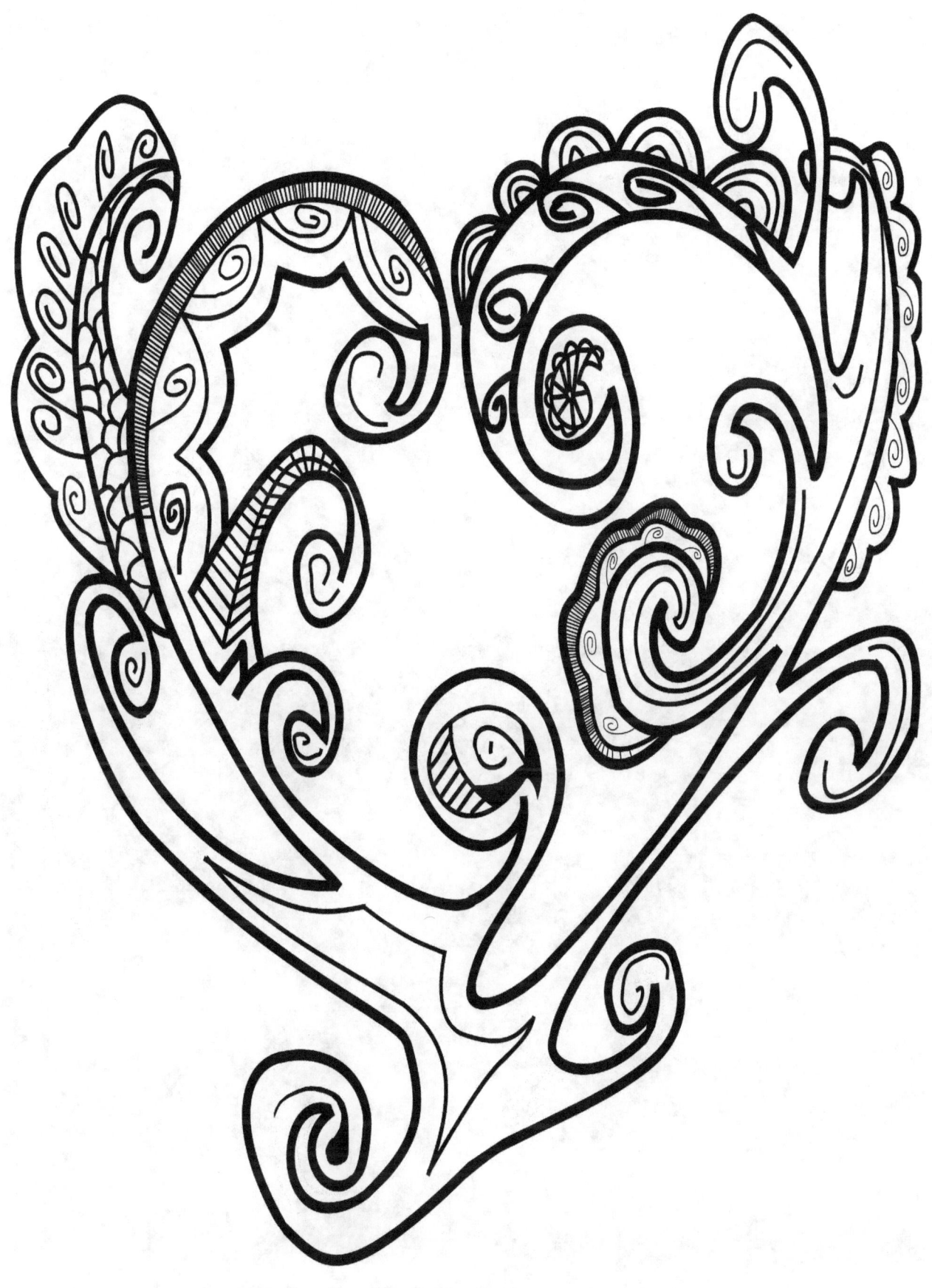

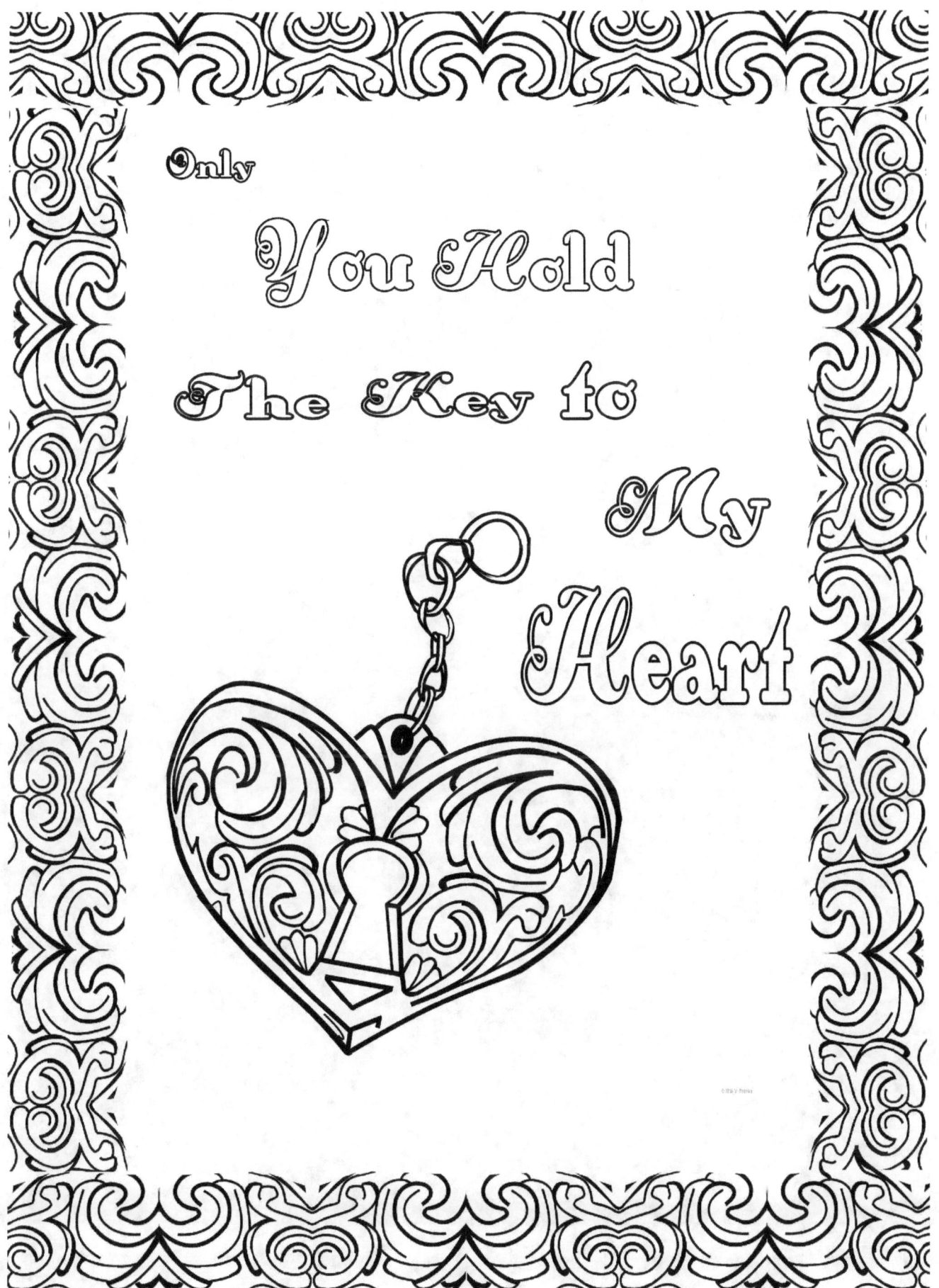

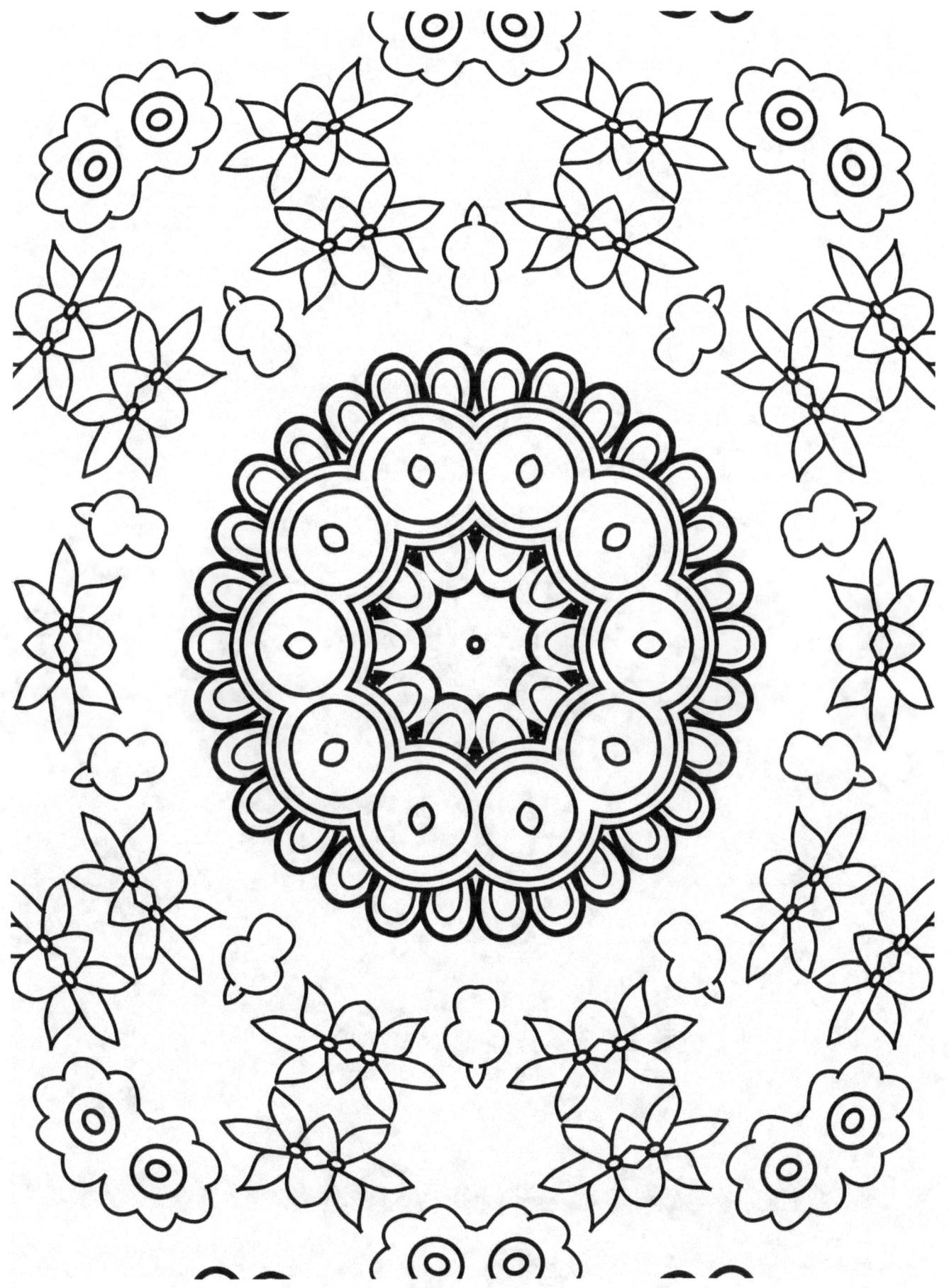

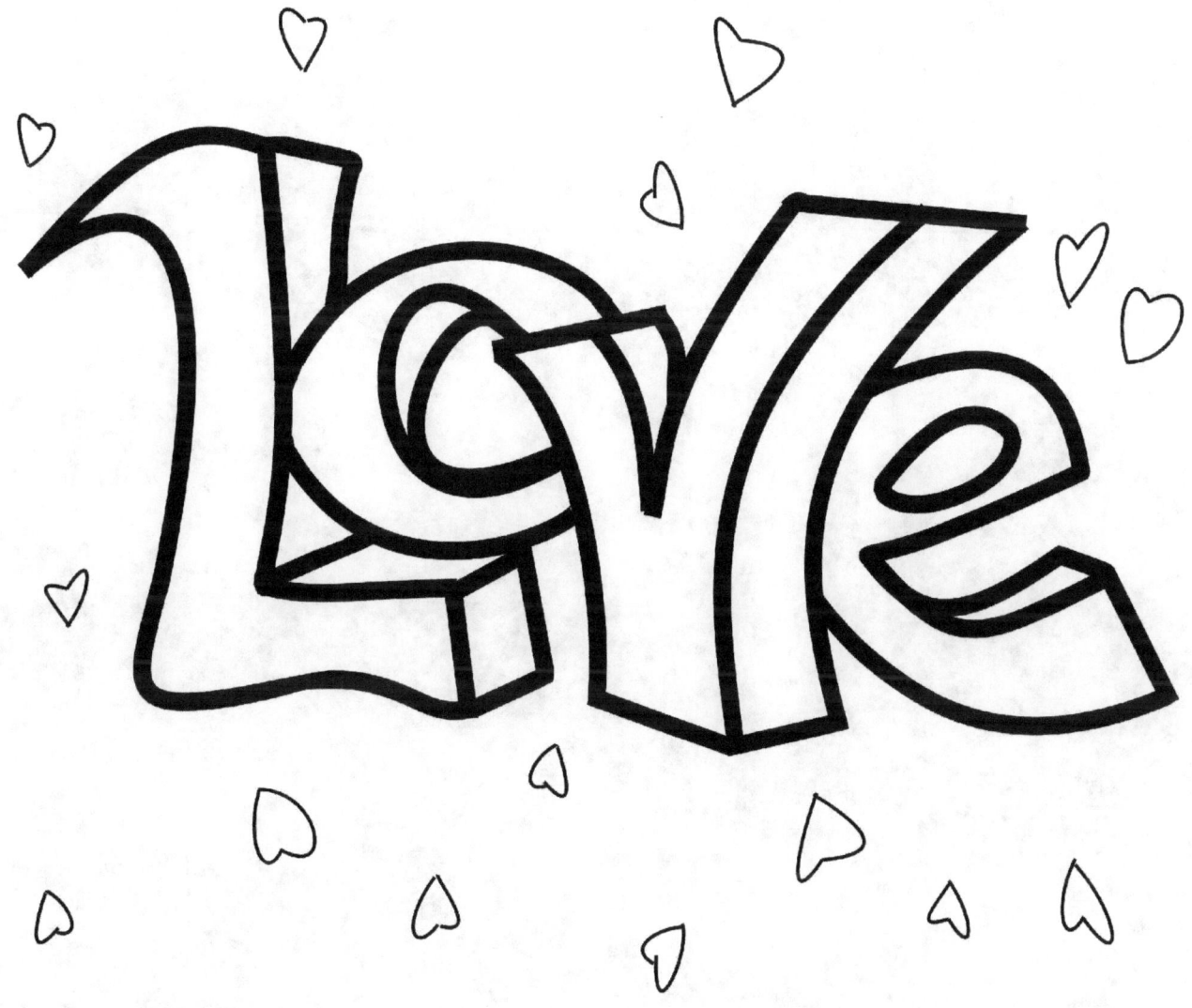

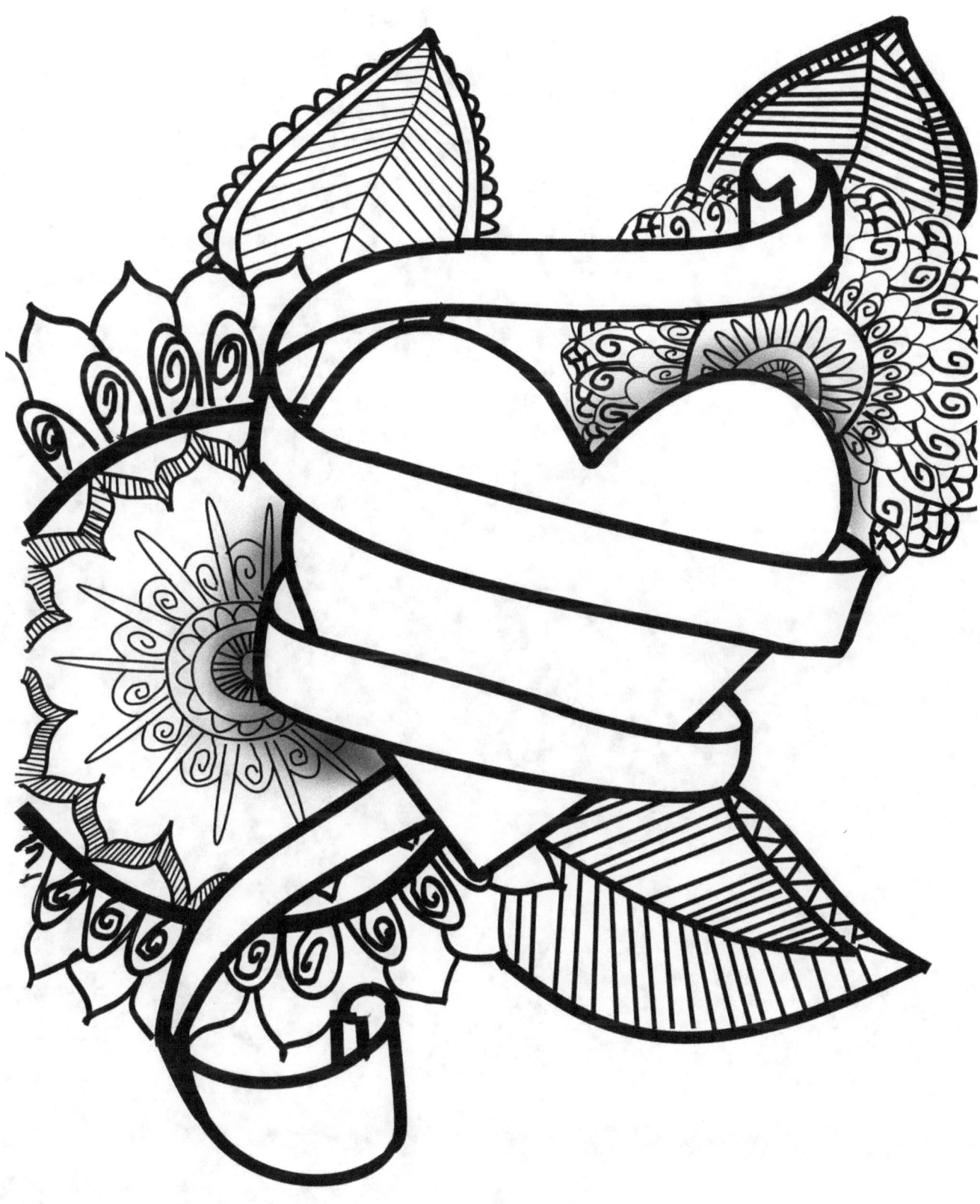

A Rose speaks of Love silently in a language known only to the Heart

You're the Smile on my FACE AND THE Beat to my Drum

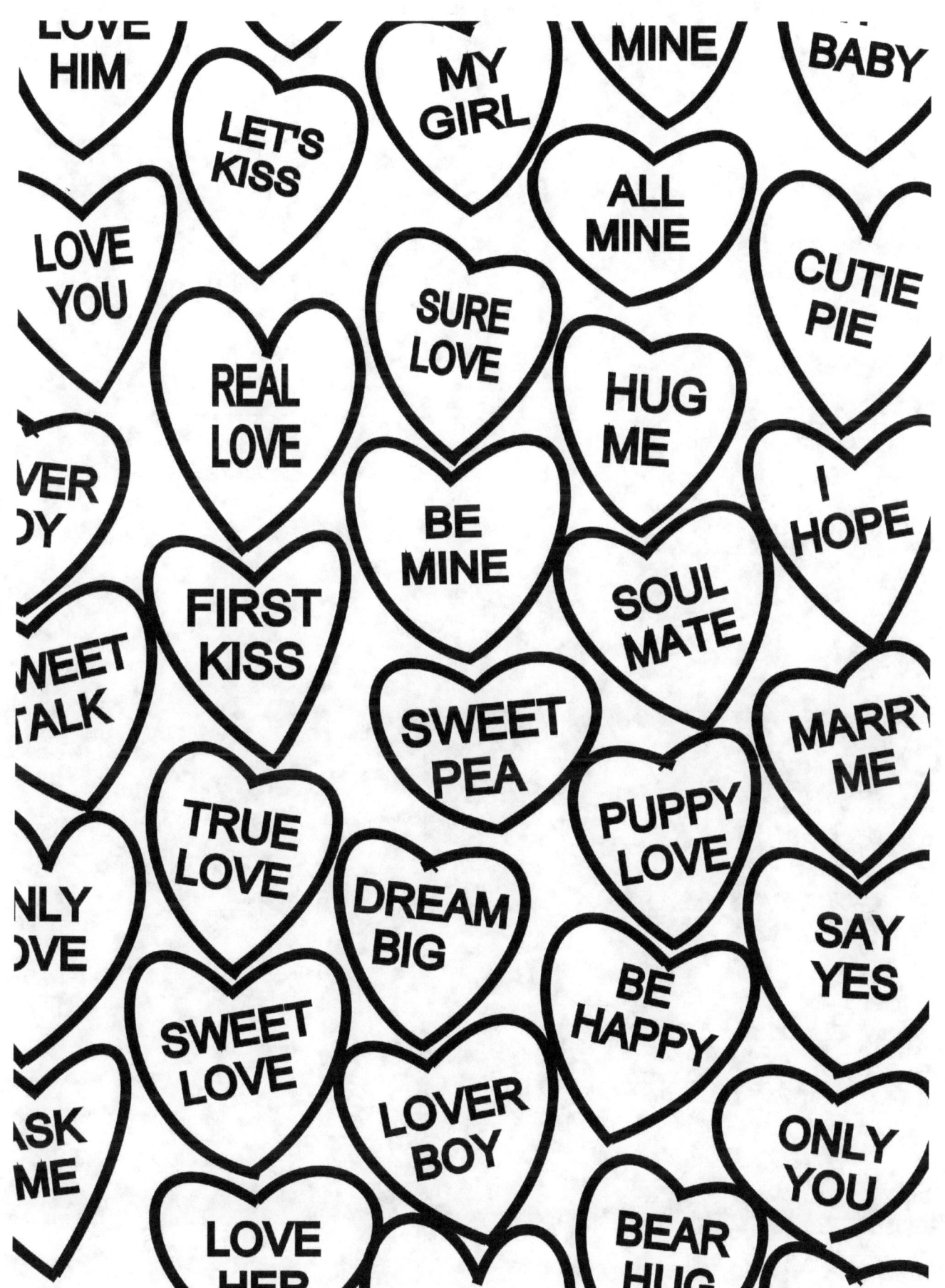

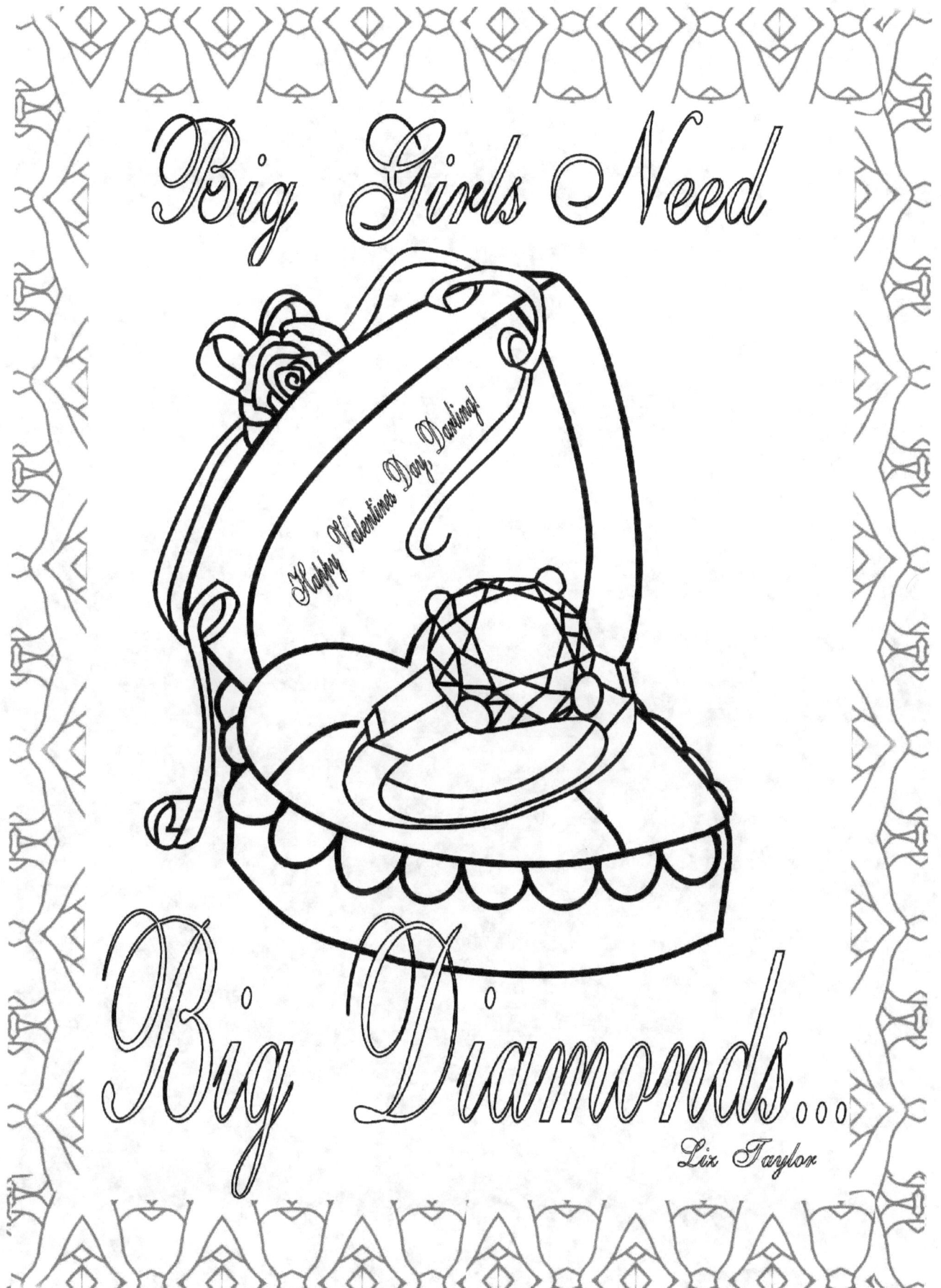

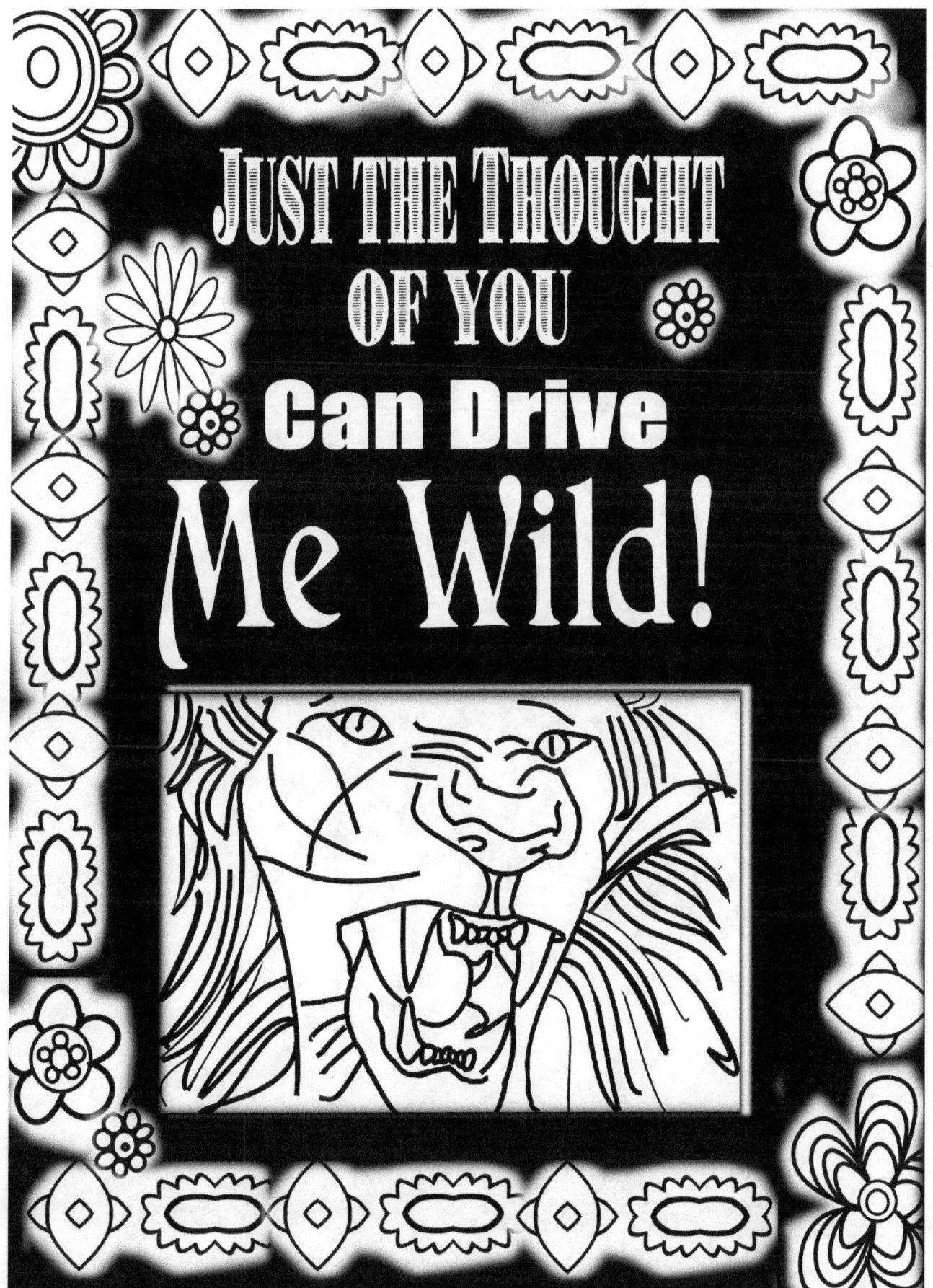

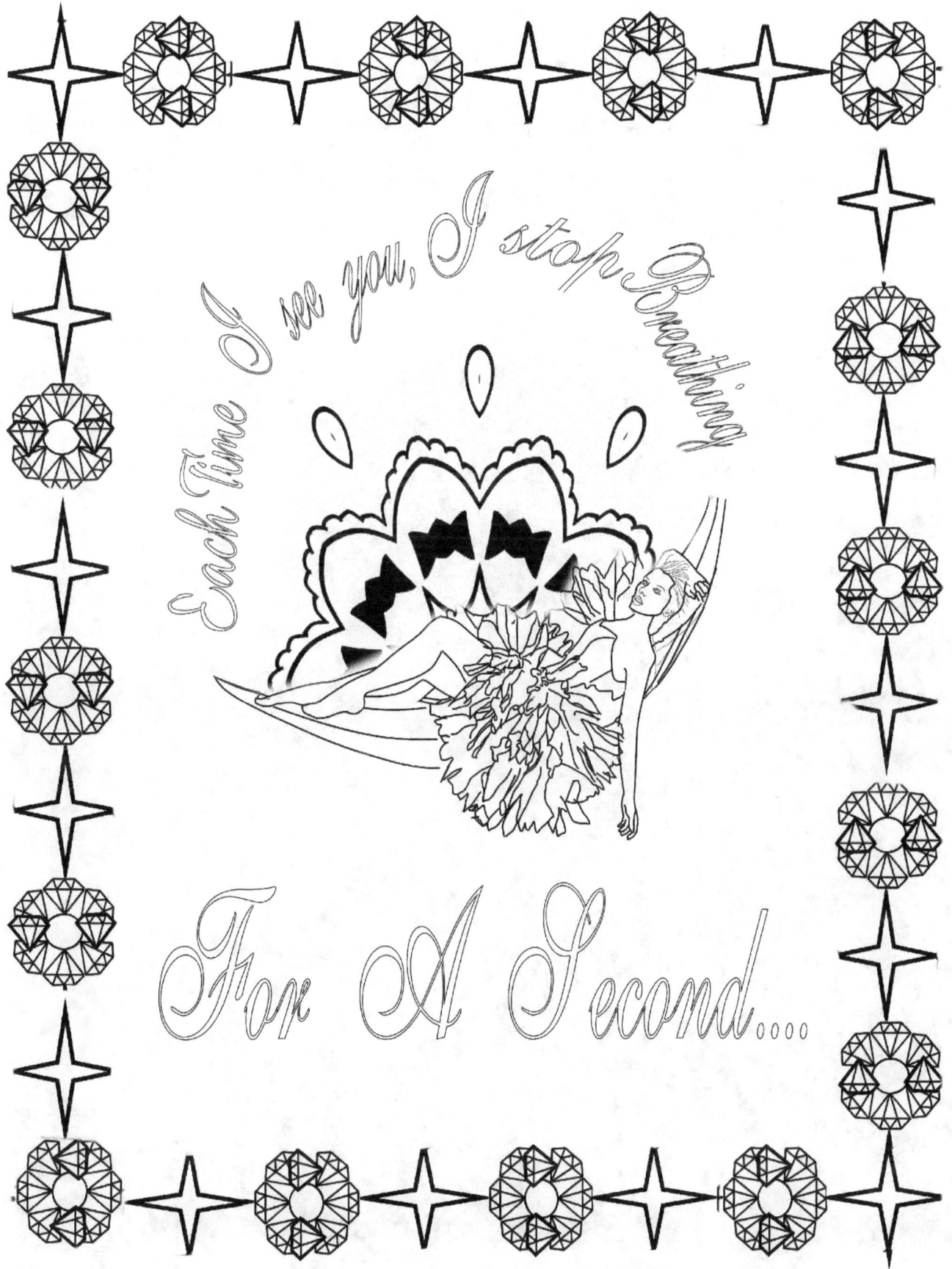

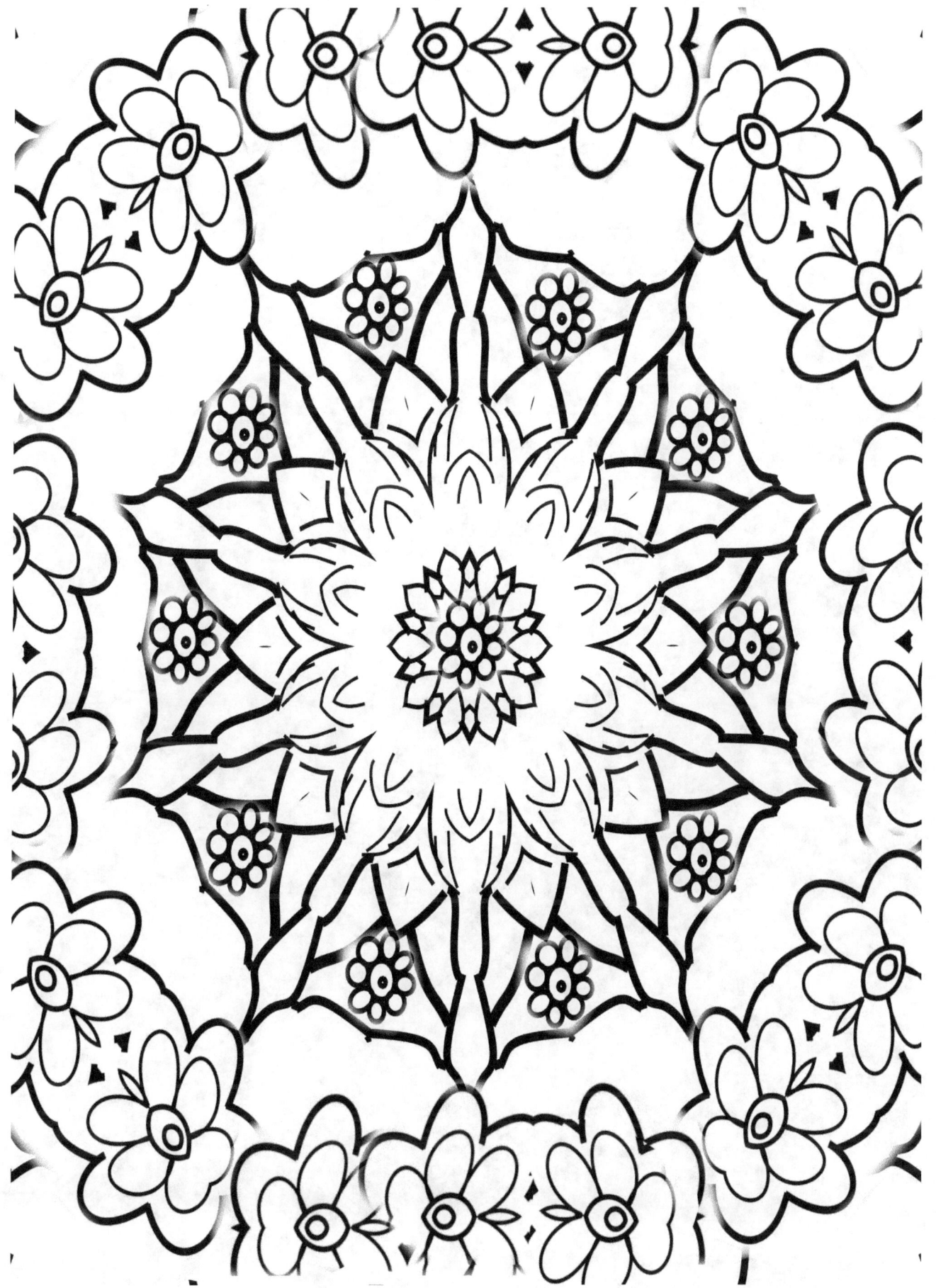

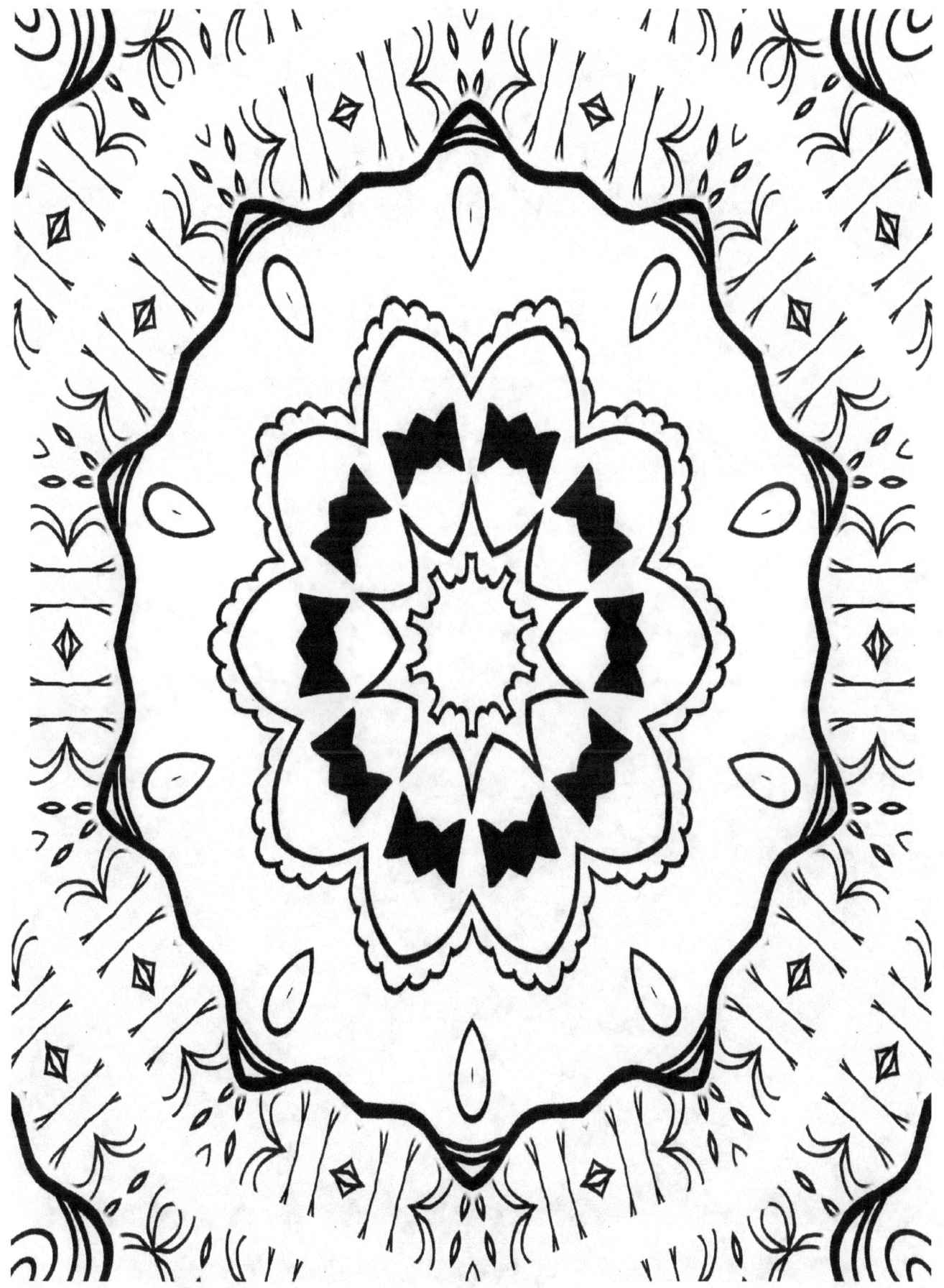

You be the KING, And I'll be the QUEEN... And we'll live Happily Ever After!

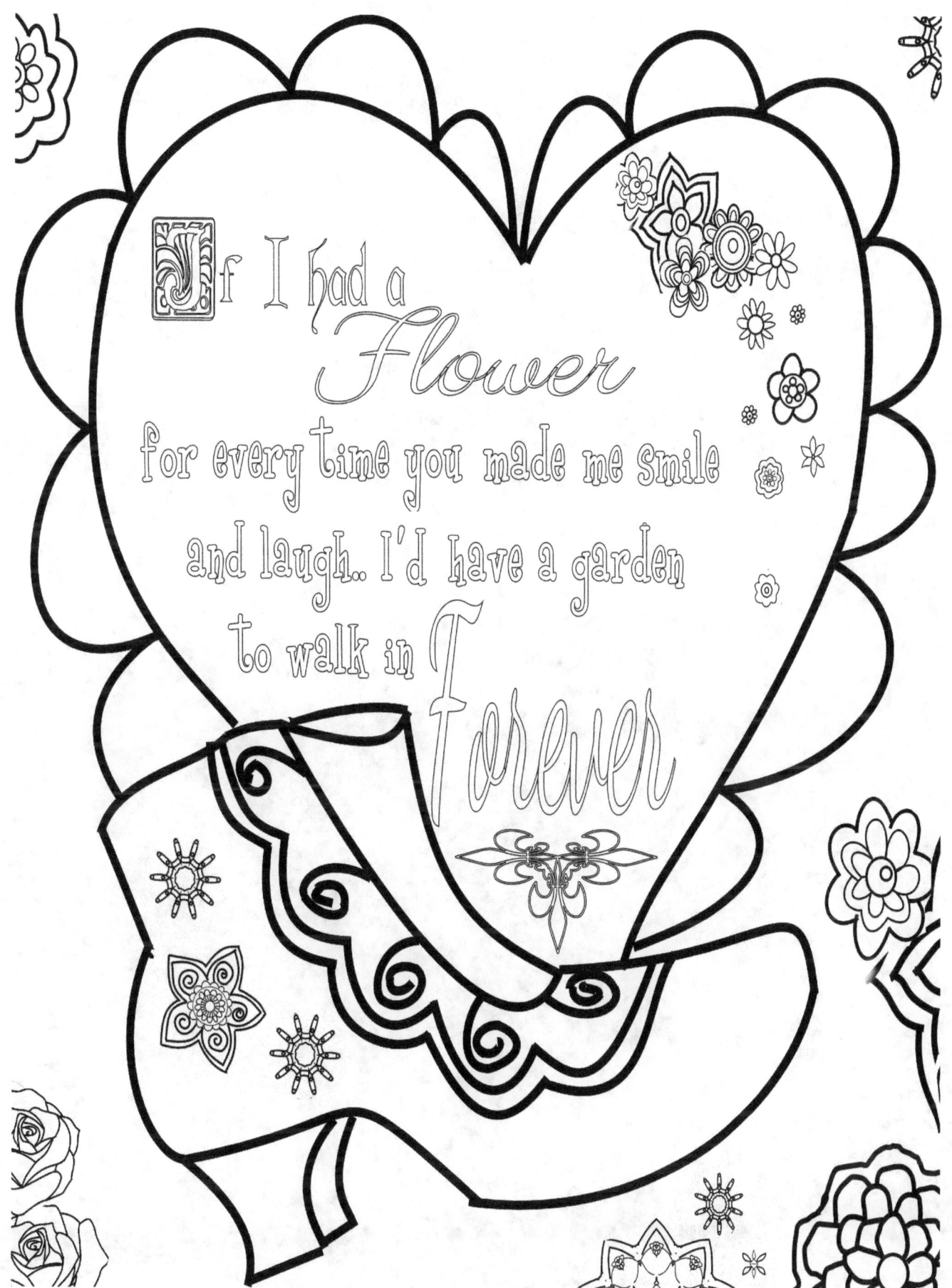

If I had a Flower for every time you made me smile and laugh.. I'd have a garden to walk in Forever

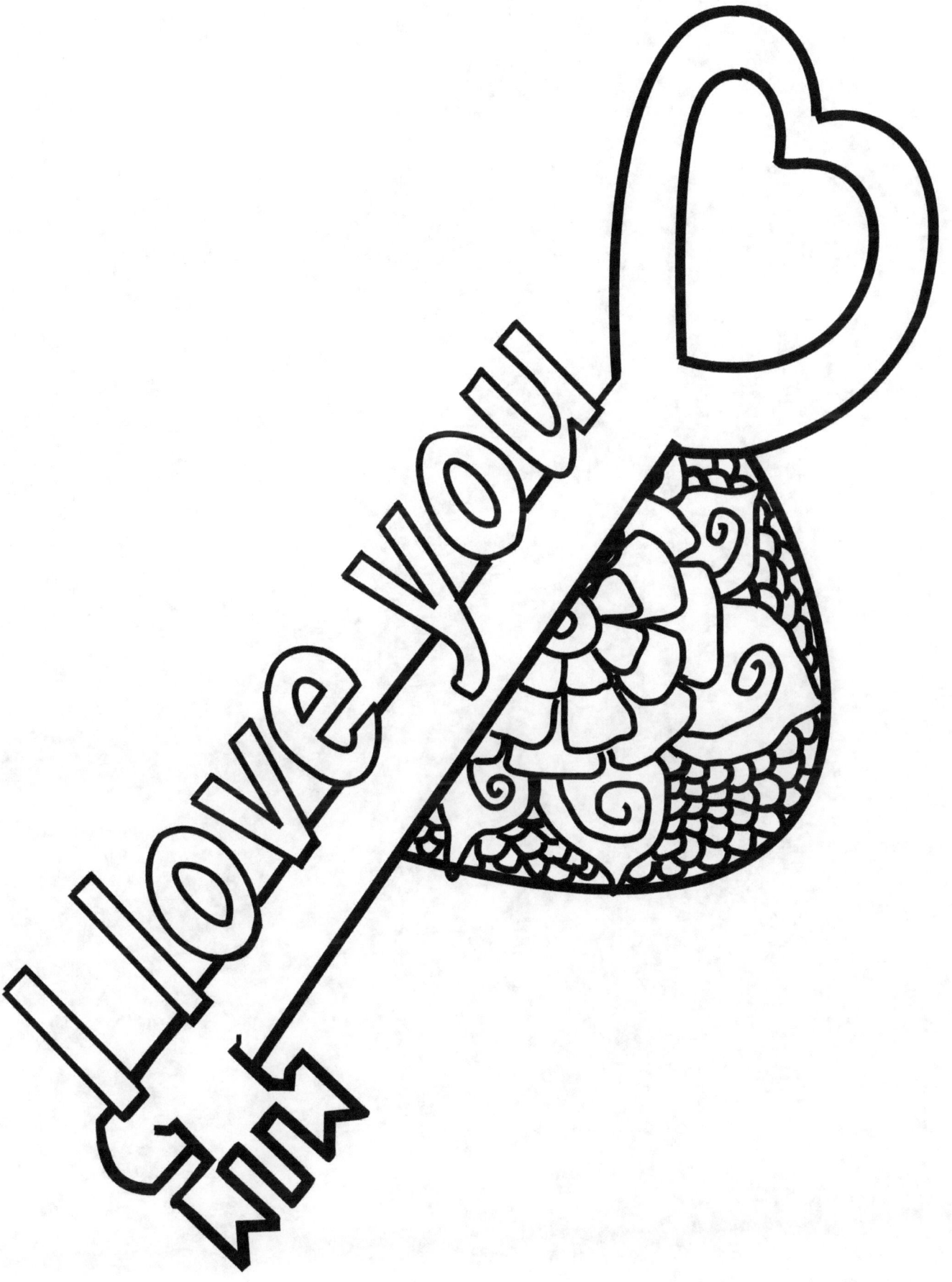

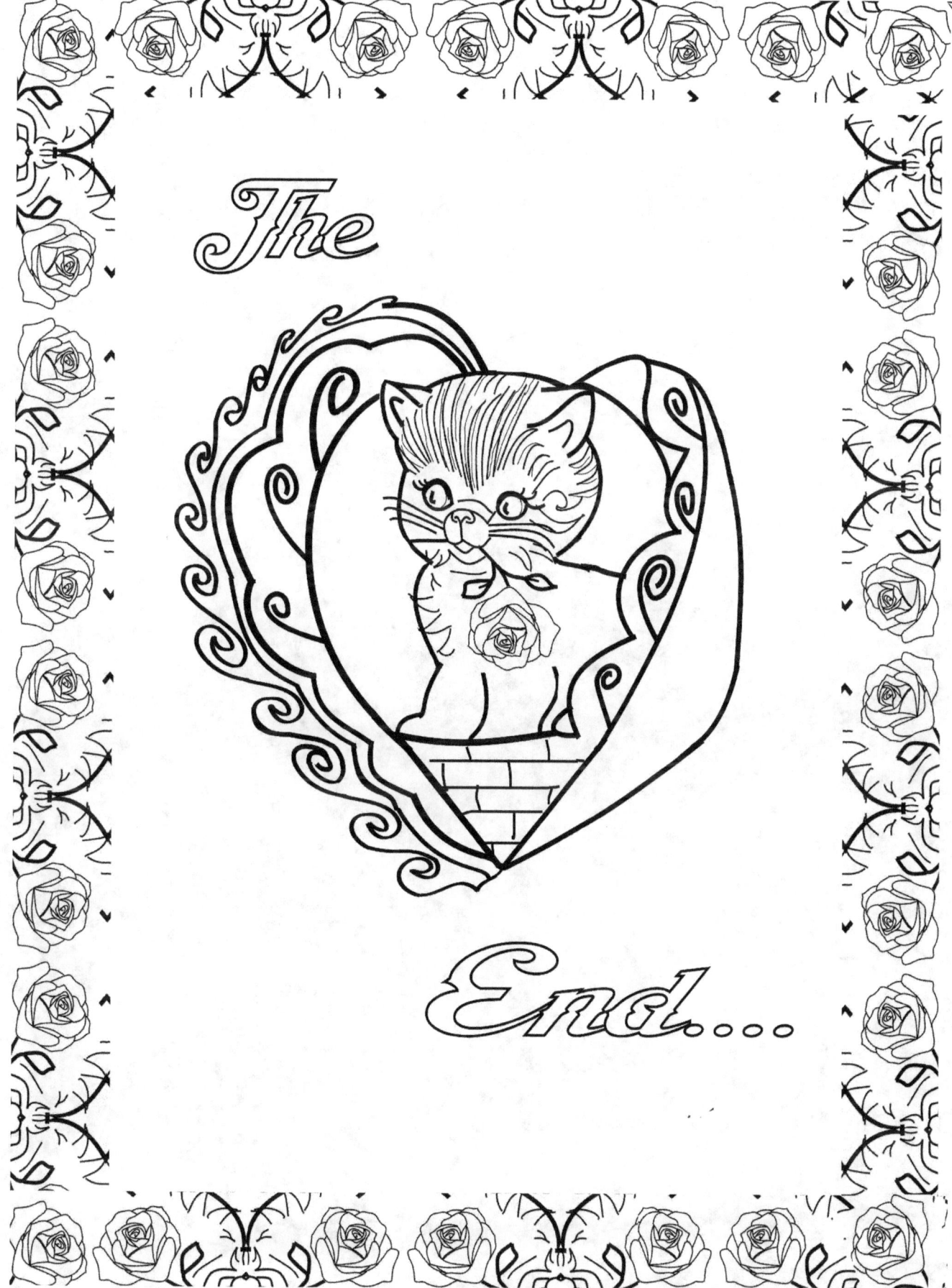

www.ingramcontent.com/pod-product-compliance
Lightning Source LLC
Chambersburg PA
CBHW081301180526
45170CB00007B/2524